RAYMOND FILIP

RIVERS
APPLAUD
FOREVER

**GUERNICA
EDITIONS**

TORONTO – BUFFALO – LANCASTER (U.K.)
2019

Michael Mirolla, editor
Cover and interior design: Errol F. Richardson
Cover photo: The St. Lawrence River as seen from
Parc des Rapides in LaSalle, Quebec
Front and back cover photos:: Delia Gurrea Filipavicius
Guernica Editions Inc.
1569 Heritage Way, Oakville, (ON), Canada L6M 2Z7
2250 Military Road, Tonawanda, N.Y. 14150-6000 U.S.A.
www.guernicaeditions.com

Distributors:
University of Toronto Press Distribution,
5201 Dufferin Street, Toronto (ON), Canada M3H 5T8
Gazelle Book Services, White Cross Mills
High Town, Lancaster LA1 4XS U.K.

First edition.
Printed in Canada.

Legal Deposit – First Quarter
Library of Congress Catalog Card Number: 2018956522
Library and Archives Canada Cataloguing in Publication
Filip, Raymond, 1950-, author
Rivers applaud forever / Raymond Filip.

(Essential poets series ; 258)
Poems.
ISBN 978-1-77183-360-8 (softcover)

I. Title. II. Series: Essential poets series ; 258

PS8561.I535R58 2019   C811'.54   C2018-905162-0

RIVERS
APPLAUD
FOREVER

ESSENTIAL POETS SERIES 258

Canada Council   Conseil des Arts
for the Arts   du Canada

ONTARIO ARTS COUNCIL
CONSEIL DES ARTS DE L'ONTARIO
an Ontario government agency
un organisme du gouvernement de l'Ont

Canadä

Guernica Editions Inc. acknowledges the support of the Canada Council
for the Arts and the Ontario Arts Council. The Ontario Arts Council
is an agency of the Government of Ontario.

We acknowledge the financial support of the Government of Canada.

This book is dedicated to my wife Delia;
my little princess Denice; and in loving memory
of my mother Bena; grandmother Emilija;
and godmother Rita Kavolis.
*   —endless light years of love*

Contents

Pocketful of Picks

Stray Birds for Unwanted Children in a Lost World

A Waterfall Sings, Not Cries

Rivers Applaud Forever

The small voice of *La Petite Rivière St. Pierre*
Speaks through tunnels, funnels, runnels, echoes …
This missing river, a fluency,
Runs beneath mean streets and green streets,
Joggers and cyclists keeping pace beside tide race
And the uproar of rapids both a song and a lasting ovation.
While at Meadowbrook golf course,
A water trap, a remember-me mire,
Scrambles on, last view of the *St. Pierre.*
A runner up.

Memory: a questing estuary.
So easy to forget
That our bodies too
Are mostly water;
Explorers of the interior;
Hearts as divided and mingling
As the Hochelaga Archipelago.
The highest falls, the most soothing counsellors:
Niagara, Montmorency, Chaudière—
Their cascades reach out with rainbow arms.
The givers amid the takers:
The settled Saguenay, and the flooding Yamaska.
The freezing, the warming, the shape shifting,
The silent clap to clay of the Champlain Sea:
In the hands of diviners,
Read the briefings of time.

St. Lawrence freighters, belugas, wind surfers,
Or Iroquois first splashers,
The cheer of a river, a mouth,
Recurrently says in one glance,
Or a trance: *enchanté*.
All my springs are for you.

Kateri Tekakwitha

Your story is a curiosity, braided corn,
Suspended and impossible to unravel.
I believed in you, once, as an empty figure,
An icon to flesh out in a colouring book.
Your people, the mohawks, had thrown stones at your backbone,
Because you had traded the drum, the dreamcatcher, the eagle feather,
Marriage and the beading circle,
For a rosary.

Smallpox, also brought by missionaries,
Infected your meek cheeks,
Your Hail Mary vision.
What did you see?
A giant turtle,
As big as an island,
Dying on its back?
What did you feel,
Kneeling in the snow?
Cold, hungry, lost,
Blazing a trail of crosses?
Did you hate men?
The smell of hell in them?
Were you a bitter virgin,
Sleeping alone with your saviour,
On a bed of pine needles?
Did you taste his body and blood
In the wine and wafers?
Can you hear these words
From the silence of your tomb?

I glory in the sanctuaries of relict rocks,
The scriptures of tree lines and shorelines,
The luxury of light that is non-geocentric,
Here long before shamans and blackrobes
Ever cast their shadows in the clearings,
Bearing False Face Masks, or man-made bibles,
To deliver us from evil.

I enter your shrine,
Beneath the blue halo of this Earth,
For no reason beyond the miracles in your name.

Kateri Tekakwitha:
Touch me, again.

Black Crosses

Cancer. It's happening to me:
"A fast, aggressive, high-risk" invasion.
Am I dying? Am I next?

"*Numéro 67!* Number 67!"
A nursing assistant,
An angel with a needle,
Sharpshoots my blood into a vial,
One emergency at a time.
"Don't move." She smiles.

Bumped up the list for an urgent biopsy, I don't budge,
As hollow-core needles poke check my prostate.
Ten spanks inside my rear end: the artist's entrance.
How many hitch knots of tumours are proliferating inside there?
The proctologist punctuates the ultrasound with a perfunctory:
"Don't move."

A sick stick,
Cancer is shrinking me, damn fast, in its submission hold.
Hands clenched, strapped down, wrapped up in a winding sheet,
I lie dead still for sixty minutes inside the Optima NM/CT 640,
An oncological dreadnought. Radioisotope tracers
Race through bone loss as brittle as bamboo.
This could be the lid of a coffin, as a scanner closes in, silently;
Camera reaping, quantifying, localizing, nearer, and nearer,
Photobombing a skeleton breathing normally …
Until a tomographic cross hits the tip of my nose.
Don't move.

And please don't tell me that wasn't an angel in a blue gown,
Leaving the restricted area of a treatment room;
Her chemo not working, her head bald,
Her eyes gracious,
Her Paclitaxil lips as pink as an hibiscus,
Whispering in my ear: "I kept the table warm for you."

We, the cancer bearers, come and go, visitants,
Passing through irradiation, RapidArc doses of hope.
Tri-monthly injections of Zoladex work their wizardry.
My pubic hair disappears, chest hirsuteness stolen.
Too much testosterone that I should bottle and sell.
Extra-strength forgiveness of enemies becomes easier—
(Though it was never in the prescription.)
Less states of denial, more sudden sweats,
Clash with the anarchy of insomnia and nausea.
I flip through sports channels to keep my mind off death.
After hearing an infomercial for therapeutic chants,
A charming dream occurs as clear as molecular imaging:
Ugly androgen receptors mutating into thousand-petalled lotuses.

"Look! There's a double rainbow!"
My wife beams with joy,
As we drive home from the hospital, one rainy evening in November.
Dead leaves everywhere: brown, or blood-in-urine yellow and red.
In the living room, she slumps over her laptop,
Exhausted from searching for natural cures;
Our love bond stronger than any clonogenic cancer cell.
She insists upon visiting the Oratory,
And reciting the "never fails" novena.
Solemnly, one everlasting twilight,
I watch the widow in her light candles,
Lame flames expiring beside a mountain of crutches.

A miracle cure for cancer?
Malignancy does not adhere to Anglican,
Or terrorist cell divisions.
The crab in a night sky
Points away from the child I cannot let go,
On what could be her last Father's Day.
My mother is still alive. Don't die for her sake.
I harbour little faith in nanobots.
Go buy a bag of *guyabanos*:
The needles in their skin, a welcome touch.
Dabble in the abracadabra of an instant green moustache,
While sipping this soursop, pureed, fried, or mystified.
Add humour, an uncanny fortifier, to the onco-heave-ho.
I swing my kettle bell, and *la vie est belle*!

Metastasis in my bones and lymph nodes
Should have begun—
But never did.
Undetectable finches sunbathed along an exit sign
In the autumn light,
When I had finished my 36 rounds of radiotherapy,
The cancer stopped at stage T2X,
Black crosses washed off my thighs.
Shine on, external beam
Of linear accelerator 21 B:
A proven saviour.
PSA now down
For the count
From 58
To 0.13.
Don't move.

Mourning Doves in Autumn

Too soon.
A trio of doves,
Heads bobbing in unison,
Coo in the dying dawn
Of another equinox.
Too soon.

Grey, brown, and so blue,
May these mournful birds
Safely cross the russet sunsets.
Missed.

The leaves of summer,
So full of chlorophyll,
Bursting with a green sheen,
Now yield and fall,
As the chills of autumn slam doors shut.

I cling to life more tightly
Than tree rings that bind heartwood.
Tracing the ecliptic,
My arms go gossamer.

The Earth wears its wardrobe of wars,
As the days grow shorter,
Less time to be innocent,
More darkness for the forgotten.

The winds are pallbearers
Of a world that will never blossom.

Autumn Taught Him

The grave won't betray me, play dice in the dark with my rest.
As the autumn trees grow spaces, I'll be a host and a guest.

Some men make big waves drowning; some leave ripples at most.
I stand, pre-deceased, objecting the least, an eschatological ghost.

Not ready to exit, not ready to go into the ground;
Fill up this minute, the infinite in it, as the heavens cool down.

The saints and big tippers, the subatomic trekkers have all had their say.
All shrines are improvised. Eternal silence can wait one more day …

Breath, Bequeathed

To whomever survives me,
As family, friends, detractors—
Or undecided:
Let's go halves.

Regrets? None.
I leave behind a clean stage.
It was a pleasure to have served
As an adopted father
For a little princess of a niece,
As we made musical waves together,
Circling our water-dipped fingertips
Around the rim of a glass, half-full.
We two were as one as the star
Inside a blue-daddy petunia.
And to a displaced family tree,
I passed around great-great grandpa's 999
Herbal liqueur invention to unite us again.
Born screaming, die singing.

As far as eternity goes,
The "heat death" of this macrocosm
Should not hinder my transmigration
Into the liege of a non-empirical realm,
Beyond decimal places. Maybe.
DNA dated within The Sixth Great Extinction:
A living liquidation, I postponed,
By half a second, through non-profit labours.
Yet the years sparkled on, and spilled over,
As rewarding as victory champagne.
This is the peace I will take with me.

Death has journeyed a long way too:
From skulls in the slime to dolmens to diamonds out of ashes;
From myths to theories to half-truths to almost there ...
Will Jesus and Marilyn Monroe
Show up on time at the Omega Point?
Maybe.

All together in a paleoecological elimination dance,
Bury half of my ashes
Under the altar of this Earth:
I and its orbit, eccentric.
Let your right hands disperse the other half
Upon living waters to ease your mourning.
Spread out this man of many parts,
Bisected by fulfillment and departure,
Well-being and non-being.
Allow metaphysical me to swim
With the angelfish and the sharks
In the single-celled divisions of the seas;
At one with the diving birds
That see beneath the surface,
And the wind shadows that shimmer
Across an unexplored shore
While the last waves disappear to be no more.

No maybe's.
As good as breath, bequeathed,
We will fare well,
On the side of love
In the symmetry of forever.

A Moon for Venus

Harvesting moonbeams,
As autumn nights fall,
I pick out Venus
With my naked eye.
She flares, a warning signal,
A hot temper, moonless, barren,
Approachable but untouchable.

Blow a kiss toward the lava flow
Of Aphrodite Terra,
The volcanic lowlands of Guinevere Planitia,
Where probes entered her atmosphere,
Landed, and disintegrated in minutes.

Space, dark energy, embrace us,
Coldly but gently in this universe;
Bound by gravity, electromagnetism,
The weak and strong nuclear forces—
And rare sightings of lovestruck eyes
That glow as radiantly as the skies.

Surfer's Eye

My wife smiles with the look of love
Through the growth across her left cornea:
A pterygium, the size of a baby oyster.
Surfer's eye: permanent damage
From wind and sun in the Visayas.
Her vision beholds the asymmetry of my anatomy
As "*gwapo*," handsome, her white husband.
And I don't see a woman of colour.

I search her irises,
Dark and bottomless as the hidden falls of Tinago,
Where we honeymooned, vigilant,
Not to step on snakes along the jungle lookout.
The dive-defying waters tumbled so invitingly,
As we swam, ooolala, the falls in our eyes.
I didn't feel the wedding ring slip off my finger,
And vanish into the deep on that magical day in Mindanao.

No sneaky snakes sleeping in my socks,
What is she imagining now?
Peeping through my (not-so-hot) e-mail,
Or Facebook, unfriending women
Who request to be my friends.
She has dumped all the grimy video cassettes,
And snapshots of ex's who once fell into my life.
A leash, a microchip, a motion detector,
May prevent my gaze from wandering.
Her two eyes suffocate
With a reach longer than two arms.
I can spy all the men who have hurt her.

The condition can never be cured,
Attachments that won't go away.
We have remained together despite
Prolonged exposure to our imperfections.

A kiss at sunrise corrects our focus
Through the morning mucus.
Four older eyes possess clearer insights;
Much, much, more sensitive to the light.

Waiting for Fireflies

These teeny luminaries

locate my dazzlement

their language of light

speaks with sparks

as random as creation

bioluminescence
hovers
here
above
climbing roses   and over there

below

a waterless waterfall

where leaves from last autumn

overflow

catch sight of

zig

zag

brilliance

befriending

my bare toes

with their glows

peewees

as carbon

once

emerged

how humans too

I can see

left brain

right brain

stardust epiphanies

luciferin fireworks

scintillate

and mate

summer flings

one life

one flash

winks

that awaken

my eyes

and sense

of direction

Space Tourist

Where to get away from the grey of every highway?
The Kármán line—where outer space begins.
An upper, nowhere close to the simulations,
More fun than skydiving or bungee jumping,
Who can resist the pull of accelerating g-forces
Tearing at heart muscles?
Or killer views of debris in a cold galaxy?
No warmer weather to look forward to,
No waters to wade in,
No spa in space,
The ability to taste and smell will wane as fishsticks
Float away inside the ultimate revolving restaurant.
Six minutes of singing somersaults for recreation:
Wheeeeee! Weightless kneeling,
Window to toe, worth the ascent.
A vacancy filled in a void,
Observers from the capsule,
An orbiting Sistine Chapel,
Can click pictures as testaments,
And incline a forefinger downward:
Godlike.

Earthbound.
A fiery re-entry, as if returning to a gift,
A hometown touchdown,
Will permit astro trotters to discover
Their land legs again,
Deprived but broadened
By visiting a vacuum museum,
Seeing more than Odysseus ever saw.

Book early for Air Miles specials across pioneer trails.
Enjoy the shopping at a commercial-crew mall,
Where extraterrestrial litter, lunar rocks, meteorite gems,
Or key chains, await the curious in sight of memorials to war.
Magnify the magnificent through an eyeCoin-operated telescope
To hi-spy that diamond in deep space: Proxima Centauri.
A must-see.

And in the spiral bouquet of sunflowers, satellites and solar systems,
Sell the universe.

When the Skies Open Up

Don't run! What's a downpour out of nowhere?
Take in the lightning with eyes shut tight.
Hear wet exclamation points splatter from smiting winds
That blow all forecasts, and introverted umbrellas, inside-out.
Taste water from above, born over and over, to fulminating thunderclaps.
Swirl with the carousel of raindrops circling in a swimming pool.

Suddenly, it's sunny.
Breathe in the freshness, the transformation.
This kind of day in the Levant must have limned the Garden of Eden;
Or the Bardo in Tibet, as serpents slid through mud and mercury,
And a morning fog lifted over fruits of gold for elixirs.
Prophecy inside alchemy inside meteorology.

Stages of Sleep

Sleep:
The blackout
That turns on
Everything …
A tuning in
Begins
With the patter
Of alpha waves.
The brain,
An electrical instrument,
Plays melodies
Never heard before;
Or recovers
From a blindness
With rapid eye movements
In delta sleep,
Where dreams and nightmares
Enter.
A 90-minute show, nightly,
Revolves upon stages of slumber.
Fall endlessly, fly, or even die.
Then return, refreshed,
Struck by lightning:
Words, music, stories,
Remembered vividly,
For the waking world.

Streets That Follow You

Dirt Path. DP Camp

Salute without remembering:
The *Lübeck-Vorwerk, Artillerie Kaserne*;
The chapel in the barrack where you weighed in
A hair heavier than your baptismal blue ribbon.

There, there, your first footsteps are gone with the British Zone;
The displaced persons in the wake of a war that will never go away.
Your parents had met fleeing Lithuania in a blur of rubble and forest.
Your mother, a farm girl, was running from her enemy, a stepmother
Who beat her, and refused to feed her, while Stalingrad burned in the snow.
Your father, from a medical family, always washing his hands,
Came of age as a black marketeer who was caught with contraband.
He had stood arms akimbo, the imperious man-about-the-DP camp,
Supplying chocolates for his children—and for his wife: a mink stole;
Goods smuggled out of the traffic in tommyrot at the docks.
A suitcase full of Export A's, Gitanes, Lucky Strikes:
The only real currency worth more than the Reich Mark.
This was liberation: detained for nine years, longer than the war.
The barbed wire went. The *dypukai* stayed. Gangplanked.
Always non-preferred, always lice-free under homburgs and scarves,
Always lower than livestock, herded off the ship
And into the dirt of port cities: Lübeck, Kiel, Halifax.

You left behind an extremity,
A newborn wrist stained with a birthmark.
Medical malpractice took that healthy hand,
Then deboned, deviated, paralyzed and atrophied
The entire arm of a DP (despised person) infant.
A twig now dangles inside your sleeve,
A souvenir.
A minor limb loss,
As they say at the Red Cross.

The past is a Destroyer,
Miniaturized inside a wine bottle for decor.
Moored to this moment,
Exercise and exorcize.
Stretch out two unequal arms.
Auf Weidersehen, baby!

Your short arm
Makes lesser men
Feel smaller.
Better-abled,
And embraceable,
Why were you born?

To be life worthy of life.

Holy Cross Street

The world began here.
Your first memory:
Our Lady Gate of Dawn.
Her Lithuanian rays opened up
An inheritance that will never reject
A sense of reverence no more
Than the Baltic sea can refuse to toss
Amber offerings along its shores.

Praise the warmest *alleluia* from a choir
That too often outnumbers the congregation.
Count the blessings as plentiful as spiraea blossoms
That surround the church within the hold of spring.
Rejoice in respect for the living and the dead.

From the brightness and rightness of amber windows,
To the lamps along the nave that reflect upon the pews,
To the candles that illuminate a Roman Catholic altar,
To the sunshine that enters through a consecrated door,
This descent of light built you, a circle of celebrants,
And so much more.

Atwater Tunnel

You enter the illuminated socket of a death skull,
Downhill on a bicycle, playing *Chase Your Echo*:
"Oooo eee ooo ah ah ting tang walla walla bing bang …"
A carophony entombs races with Chevies and faces on the 107 bus,
Chokeholds of weeds in walk-fast walkways that infest nightmares,
To a marketplace where flower ladies stand rooted with cement smiles.
The popsicle sticks in the spokes of your wheels speak about seeing
Too much, too quick, as you rip along an arsonist's arse of rowhousing;
The ABC's of F'ing off with graffiti.
Make your spit mark and die.
Or … escape … slowly … from Verdun tunnel vision—
And a family falling apart with the dripping tar.

"*Ne, papa!*" Your sister shrieks in bed,
As the smiling hebephile feels her up,
Smitten by sex kittens in her teen-zines,
And her frugging cleavage.
Sunday night incest, Father Knows Best.
"*Ne, papa*," you whimper,
As your old man, a lugan with a gun,
Aims his Pinkerton pistol at your sleeping head,
At his wife, at his daughter, at his battered ones.
He threatens to murder you all,
Once he comes home from the night shift.

Fight back with all the fury
Of a thousand generations.
Don't cry along the aqueduct,
As sullen as a sealed tunnel.
The bully boys mock your biodiversity:

"Hey ugly! What happened to your arm?"
Should you be the polite lamb chop?
Or hit 'em with spitfire wit?
"Make a fist." Doctor's orders.
Be twice as good.
Crush that condescension
With the confidence of a jackhammer.
Earn some bragging rights,
Your cup of humble hubris.

Up and down Atwater, inner-city Sisyphus,
The sewers swear at you *chrrriss d'Calvaire*,
On this *colline* de sin: Notre Dame, St. Jacques, St. Antoine.
Sacrement, tabernacle, mon hostie, j'ai eu un flash!
Your faith sways like a rosary
On a rear-view mirror.
See black people, defaced, invisible too.
They don't talk down to you.
More comfortable with them,
Hitchhike to Harlem,
Lenox Avenue, the last Renaissance.
Hear what's comin' round the intersection.
The traffic lights don't work
But the music signals left
Before the world breaks in.
You sleep in Central Park attacking
A squished peanut-butter-and-jam sandwich.
The somebodies and the nobodies
All stroll on by as boarded-up as the buildings.
You is just another
Downtrodden dandelion.
Only the hookers and dealers
Like the x's in your eyes.

They give you the creeps.
Read a book, a true companion.
Peripatetic autodidact,
Avoid the hippies, Godot, Kerouac,
And the found pennies of ideology.
Outgrow ideas, outgrow clothes,
But how to outgrow belittlement?
Ease your weary calluses
Inside a hostel, or dumpster.
Parasites everywhere.
All cracks run crooked.
The Lincoln Tunnel,
Or the cerebral cortex,
A bum steer is a bum steer.
Surrounded by emotional cripples,
You scuff by grumpy and gauche,
As torn apart as a shredded tire,
Warped worse than asphalt,
Hubcap on your headstone.

Are you dead or alive?
What's the difference?
Every street is a dead end when you're poor:
The stabbings, the rapes, the unreported
Ends of ropes built into the darkness;
The anal canal of the Wellington Tunnel;
The hungry artery of the St. Rémi.
Hardened by Bridge Street, Charlevoix, Evelyn,
Their passageways spooky even during the day,
Ascend from this trench pattern of ruts,
As sure as the homing pigeons
You once kept as pets;
The lovely lila flying free
In a flurry of wingbeats against your heart.

Rise above red-brick-graystone-brownstone
Deadlocks of anger and despair;
The demolition circuit of back lanes, sheds,
And laundry hanging in the nothingness;
The stink of smokestacks and factory-sealed bigotry;
The rats in the walls and garbage of what's-this-piss alleyways;
The turds for flies,
And the condemned tenements for people;
The homeless beggar on the steps of an abandoned church.
Deal with this gutted reality.
Mumble to the landfill along the river,
And leave your troubles behind inside whirlpool tunnels.
Any place is better than home.

McGill College Avenue

Education empowers.
You live in the library
With the wrong crowd:
Dead authors.
English literature, a pathfinder,
May solve the maze test of existence.
Leacock 132 will get you through.
Your unpolished accent won't vanish in the halls,
But you make the grade.
Hope is a cornucopia of diplomas.
Don your graduation gown
With the honour of a prize fighter's robe.

Your dream of quiet days
In academe comes true.
You win the me, me, me,
Mêlée for a college teaching post.
Felicity in the faculty lounge:
Brie double cream, *canapés*, chardonnay,
Soup, salads and snubs beside the cold cuts—
Far better than being *paté* on the highway.

Tenured to your truth,
You drive by the breached alma mater.
Red martlets, atop the Arts Building,
Flutter over everybody's heads.
You never fail to smile
At the green grass of gravitas,
And the cracked-up sidewalk
From bursts of laughter with Louis Dudek:

Two blue-collar scholars,
Ambling arm in arm through the Roddick Gates,
Blithely in eternal conversation.

The Baltic Way

Unarmed citizens held hands across 675 kilometres:
Lithuania singing to Latvia singing to Estonia singing
To per capita euphoria!
The dance of independence upon a collapsed Iron Curtain,
"The Singing Revolution,"
We passed the audition!

That same route along Šauliai had been patrolled
By KGB police and Red Army god squads,
When you had knelt upon the floor
Of your cousin's Lada, one Soviet afternoon,
Ready to be shot, jailed, or fined,
For one peek at banned crosses,
(Fewer in number than the apostles),
Hammered into a hillside.
You were searching for the missing half
Of your Canadian voice, a lost hyphen,
The aria of the wind in the diaspora.

When the USSR dismembered itself,
Rotten as the rump of Lenin,
The hyphen from "*Kanada*" connected
With the poetry party! *Valiooooooo*!
Gladiolas, daisies, rutas,
From large audiences in small towns,
Greeted the laureates of summer.
Your clandestine screeds had earned you a seat in their minivan,
Transported exultantly as if carried on the shoulders of the people.
One highest of noons, on a country road,
Sun beams radiated off accordion keys,

As silenced voices polkaed loudly,
Gulping down eels in one slam dunk,
Vodka flowing steadily as the Nemunas river.
They inhaled deeply the fresh oxygen of freedom;
Intoxicated by speech, mobility, assembly,
Jump-over-your-own-tombstone joy!

This is what you get for believing in the unbelievable:
The fall of the Berlin Wall!
The hammer and sickle ditched with the decay of Chernobyl!
Nazism *kaputt*! Kaiser helmet pickled!
Monarchies neutered, pawns beating kings and queens!

In due time, empires will die out,
As backward as a flat Earth.
Identity is a journey, not a fixed flagpole.
One day, six continents, holding one-hundred-and-ninety-five countries,
One human chain of solidarity,
Will own the peace on one glorious home planet.

Bourbon Street

French kiss in the French Quarter
With your future bride,
Praline sweetness on her lips.
At the Café Du Monde, you stir up trouble
With the cream and sugar, enticing pickpockets.
Necking in public is prohibited in New Orleans?
Unless you slip these who dats a tip?
Too whoopee'd out, you don't suss, and say:
"No, man! You gotta pay *us* for the show!"
Just then, the manager comes whipping out,
And decks one thug with his tenderizing knuckles.

Avoid looking too innocent under the neon of Bourbon Street.
Your lady wolf-whistles at curvaceous legs that stick out of a storefront;
High heels and plaster thighs rubby rub together, man-ipulating.
Eyeballers can do some libido in there:
Slow-dance a *frottage* with any waitress,
Where the house band whacks off with whammy bars—
And awww, what a young tongue
Can do to an old perdido in the washroom.
Less treacherous to go through the red lights
Of Basin and Canal; the saloons of Storyville
Wiped away with the olden jizz of Buddy Bolden.
The wrecker's ball won all the cutting contests,
The horny tunes now corny,
The blue books on bed sheets Lulu White'd.

You pay for the past.
She'll be your sugar,
And you'll be her lemon.

Get that cocktail up, up, up into the open air!
Look, look, look, you can hold your liquor.
Through fires and floods and bursting bladders,
Swirl those hurricane daiquiris.
Taste that passion fruit.
Louisiana, *mmmmmmwah*!

Smooching and drinking
In unlimited quantities,
A pair of impaired pedestrians
Navigate the whiskey spillways,
More caboozed than the Montrealer train
That sways and chug-a-lugs
Along the Pontchartrain bridge.
Her hormones in heat,
Dance higher on Desire Street.
Strip off the tails
From shrimp and crawdad,
And suck on their heads,
A hot aroma you can eat,
Until that nightly nookie,
Licking her pit and pot.
69'd then DSM-5'd
By her dissertation, giggly pillow talk,
She psyches out Freudian "tuck-ins,"
And the madness of the world
In between sex and death,
And why you never turned out
To be a sociopath.

Fellatio for breakfast,
Keep the coitus coming,
Interrupted by a marching band.

Allez-ooop-ooop-a-dooop!
Swizzle more doubles to remain above sea level.
O say can you see your name
On the plaque at the Famous Door bar?
Below Pete Fountain and Sharkey Bonano.
You're a musicianer too!
A ragin' Canajun, eh?
With a higher calling!
"Ow! Woooooo!"
You leave the premises hollering:
"I don't want to be famous!
I just want to be ubiquitous!"
Spluttering so wild all the alligators dive bomb
Back into their swamps clear across the bayous.

Where did the week go beside the tipsy Mississippi?
Wave bye-bye from a sleeper car, and *fais-do-do*.
"*Laissez les bons temps rrrrrrrrrrrrrrrouler!*"
At sunrise, she bares her tits to Alabama,
A wet vagina leaking sperm.

You coupled for five years.
The joys of contraception
Got in the way of children.
She picked up her Ph.D in clinical psychology,
Then dropped you for a richer man like daddy.
(The no-fault divorce, a burlesque, of course.)
But that $inking $ensation began in New Orleans:
Drowning in head games,
Wickedy woo.

Interior Road, Tawid District, Poblacion Barrio

A wayside with no name follows you down,
Where *hubble-hubble* motorcycles scoot on by.
Grandma cheerful in the back, junior fast asleep in the front
On popsie's lap, momsie in the middle: a family value pack.

You go to Asia just to get out of the house.
Try to stare down the Bohol Sea …
And just when you're not looking,
A woman, a Pinay,
Really rotates your axis,
Livens up your deadpan.
She is the first person on Earth
To consider a birthday party
—For you—(surprise! surprise!)
Forty-eight-years young under the stars.
Have a clambake and cake,
On a beach where jao lizards laze as spectators,
When not multiplying.
You become a *coy-coy*,
A household elder,
No longer a cherry boy.
Pile on that domesticity.
Filipinos stick together,
As tightly as spawn,
And reef-building corals.

Survival is that cockfight into the night;
The pheromones under a full moon;

The nesting grounds on islands not drowned
By wind reversals during monsoon season.
You are a stranger barefootin' lucky in the azure,
Stepping out with the local sea goddess.
Both of you can't breathe without music in the air.
Sampaguitas love a guitar.
She swivels as only a Boholana can on land,
Dancing in sync to click-clack *tinikling* bamboo sticks.
Each day, a fiesta, somewhere, gongs and gambangs,
Whistles and drums, squealing *lechons*,
Can be heard all the way to China.
Along the main drag, an undeveloped road,
Your children will play hide-and-go-seek
Behind the short-lived petals of gumamelas.

Three summers of boom boom,
Then next comes the samba
Of one step forward,
Two steps back in Canada.
She's not the maid,
She's the lady of the house.
Holder of a Med-Tech degree,
She wipes genitalia and behinds in a bedrail jail,
Where senior snorers will never get out alive.
The remains of two married pensioners
Lie frozen in a meat locker, unclaimed—
No condolences, not even from the public curator.
She rescues an Alzheimer's nocturnal wanderer
Who trips off alarm bells to trudge through snow,
And to blather at winter haze.
Another floor, another death.
Someone's mother, disposable,
Passed away, muttering first names:

"Negotiating."
Do not resuscitate.
She cleans the corpse,
Then says a prayer for the parent
Who died alone.

Here but not here,
Her remittances to the Philippines are her presence in pesos.
Dare not go near the procession of roses, lilies, carnations,
Gerberas, dahlias, geraniums, and birds of paradise,
In her kitchen, her business, her peace, her private sector.
Unsold mums and baby's breath wither in the corner.
Her own body toddles, topsy turvy,
From the aftershock of fertility treatments,
A megadose of Femora and depression.
No embryo joyride of expectancy for her,
A Tau cross of scars kick at her womanhood.
This one, from a fibroid operation,
Cleaves her uterus.
That one, a dot, makes official,
The extraction of an ovarian cyst.

Stay loyal
To her barren depths.
Childless.
Your son, unborn.
Your daughters
Who never were.
Nameless roads
On a sunken island.

Rue d'Amour

Your mother babysteps with her walker,
Faster than the speed of darkness,
Adjusting to walls and windows for the elderly.
Her falls have brought her here:
To Rigaud, to a mountain, to sing again.

This is her home, a small room,
Simple as a convent cell, where she rules,
Content with her Ativan and parish bulletin.
Caregivers bestow the royal treatment upon her:
Breakfast in bed, a hair trim, pedicure, and chocolate whippets
The whole sweet day for her resurrected appetite.
Signatures, from the staff, blanket her birthday card;
And flotillas of balloons welcome beginnings—
Not termination.
Her new "boyfriend," a stuffed monkey,
Sleeps at the foot of the bed.
And beside the windowsill,
As bright as a party dress,
Her rejuvenated begonia
Shows off petals of orange,
That flowered from an unseen bud.

One spoonful of trepidation persists
In her long life of losses:
That she will outlive her choir,
Not one soloist remaining to intone
The *Libera Me Domine* for her.
Inexplicable how the vocal cords
Of a half-deaf, dentured, diapered,

Octogenarian can burst into song,
As pure as an angel in a blue sky
That has never known rain.

Beautiful, dutiful, chin up,
She will escort you out,
As if she owns the place,
The narrowing corridors of mortality.
Springtime lights up the sun room again,
And she watches with her goodbye eyes,
As you leave after a weekly kiss of peace.
"*Su meile, ma.*"
The exit door closes … serenely …
"*Su meile.*"

Chemin du Golf

Île des Soeurs, Alta Vista, Myrtle Beach, Osprey Valley:
Beauty points from the tees to be the best you can be.
Here at Cabot Links, Nova Scotia,
Five hours in a parallel universe, a utopia,
Awaits with the ocean whiffs off Northumberland Strait.
Golf will add years to your scorecard,
And keep the kids off the streets,
A holistic exercise
For those who find yoga too slow.

"Where you coming from?" The starter asks.
"The game of life," you give him the receipt.
Acceptance. Go walk the course.
Swing those weapons of peace that work. Bam!
The MS Fairsea landed way out there
In the Atlantic circle at Pier 21,
When you were a two-year-old waif,
Whupping pneumonia and scarlet fever,
Rocked by the January waves higher than the ship,
Cheating death by one day.
You could have arrived as a dead baby,
Decomposed by now in a Halifax cemetery.

Two haunted hands, and a wide stance,
Invite the challenge of blustering winds
That will beat you up blissfully;
Monstrous open mouths of bunkers
That will swallow golfers all day long;
Gorse and heather and angles of entanglements
In fescue grass that Pythagoras couldn't solve;

Dunes to spatter sand into spiked shoes
Soaked and baked with the smell of seaside salt;
And the rhythmic pounding of surf
As background music to inspire the perfect round.
The O of the sun, the O of the moon,
And the O of a white ball in a blue sky,
All spin in harmony with the waltz
Of your backswing to downswing to follow through,
As your feet lift off the ground, the poetry of kinesiology,
For sneaky-long distance.

Promises kept to your God, country, family and self
—(The Grand Slam)—
You hesitate to sound like an American president
But your golf game comes first.
Whatever happens next,
Armageddon or a hole-in-one,
Remember to always play within yourself,
And to visualize, holding the finish.

The Rainbow Below the Water Cannon

Myoelectric Michelangelo Hands

Serviceman, servicewoman, so uniform, all fit for body bags,
Go pawn those mickey-mouse parade gloves.
Shove those unmanned, emasculated, unconscionable drones.
You, the armless, the legless, the jobless, the aimless,
The volunteer cannon fodder for another century;
You, the blind, the deaf, the dumb from slaughtering
More civilians than foes for The Greater Good;
You, the suicidal, the xenophobic, the insensitive,
Enabled by myoelectric Michelangelo Hands:
You're so out of touch.

When the bugler plays taps,
Fall out of line.
Join ranks with the winners,
The reverse warriors
Who grasp inner peace:
(That white poppy unseen amongst the blood red).
Flash back to Ypres, 1914, The Christmas Truce.
The Germans started it, when some mother's son,
Carrying the light of dawn within him,
Crossed the firing line to shake hands,
To share holly and carols, cognac and cigarettes—
Not mustard gas;
To try on each other's headgear in a brouhaha of hah-hah-hah's—
The *avant-garde*!
To kick the stitches out of some blimey ball
That a Brit in a greatcoat had booted onto No Man's Land.
No imperial signatories, no declaration turning yellow vaingloriously,
Peace beat war.

In recognition of their *esprit de corps*, their sanity,
Their courage to obey the commands of their hearts,
Lay aside your rifles and defend Thou Shalt Not Kill.
Escalate a non-violent momentum,
From The Great Law of Peace
By Hiawatha and Deganawida to *Satyagraha*.
Promote true bravery, not the military propaganda geeks.
The Tank Man in Tiananmen Square
Who had ordered the engines of war to go away!
Standing as tall as a world leader, (not for a photo op),
He spoke for the ordinary majority in every public square,
Holding two shopping bags full of peace.

Advance with dialogue, education, universal disarmament.
Develop Earth-respecting industries for an economic boom,
Smarter than any smart bomb.
Save, not destroy, the love inherent in human nature.
That's reality too, soldier. Why love only one country?
Why mass murder as proof?

Don't stand on guard to protect
Naval vessels invaded by rust.
Might is blight.
Deter taxpayers from the Diefenbunker,
Where children spelunker for Easter eggs.
Hup two, three, four,
Flush those flying dinosaurs:
The Jurassic Sea Kings,
The not-so-stealthy CF-18s,
The Avro CF-100 Canuck "Clunk."

Row on row on row of scrap heaps
For the ruling elites, the ouchless,
Detached from the ultimate sacrifice;
Detached from microprocessor sensors where trigger fingers were;
Detached from carbon-fibre legs;
Detached from their freaking lower bodies
Doing the splits from their freaking upper bodies.
Under the blunderbuss of history,
Bury swords and sarin, warheads and joysticks in last judgment.

Whenever I see a flag,
I salute the wind.

The Wreath of Cyclical Violence

Lest we forget …
The recruit who was slain on Parliament Hill by a "crazy lone wolf"
Could also about-face into a sniping fool,
As cold as the statue he was guarding.
No one wins,
Entwined in the wreath of cyclical violence.

Horses Are Pacifists

Those four police horses,
Ears at rest, relaxed from head to hoof,
Are not Canadian bays that nicker, or kick,
Unpredictable with swishing tails to interpret.
No, they are prisoners,
Adapted to captivity, kettling, sound grenades,
Sirens, tear gas, pepper spray, rubber bullets,
Or water cannons trained on children.

My heroes have always been horses.
The Palomino that leads a parade
Rebels against unnecessary force.
Make the rider pound pepper,
The brute in the stirrups.

The Percheron that shakes off a *calèche*,
Smashing into cars that cause carnage and pollution,
Manifests a voice that needs to be heard,
A neigh sayer in upright defiance.
(Put blinders on the tourists.)

Horses, never saddled,
On Sable Island,
Romp beside breakers,
Where the ocean sprawls
Across a shifting sandbar,
And the winds of nor'easters
Comb feral manes.

No nosebag, no silver spurs,
Never measured by human hands,
Horses stand tall as peaceful animals:
The powers that free us.

Finger Pointing

I don't pretend to be an artist, or a working-class hero,
A pundit without portfolio:
No shortage of those.

I don't presume to have THE ANSWER—
A surplus of them.
You you you you you unite!

But if political correctness demands a change,
Someone to blame for the mess,
Point a finger at your mirror.

Rumble Strips

Tonight, it's the Outaouais.
Placid and toxic.
Spring has thrown away the fishing huts.
The walleye and I, this April, wished
That a caravan of pickup trucks and vans
Would all sink with the heavy metals into the river.

So ... hi-beams ... darkness ...
The righteous path has led to this,
A moment of silence for the future.
Sit down, sorrow, in the passenger seat.
We're heading toward solar wipeout anyway,
7.72 billion years down the road,
Already within visibility.
Intelligent life itself emerged from an accident:
A wrong turn of potluck particles, Goldilock glaciers.
Call it celestial mechanics, or damnation.
Evolve, then fizzle into gas and dust,
A lovely traffic fatality.

Restrain me, rumble strips, please.
So tempting to just lapse at the controls,
And to rage into those speeders out there,
Late for their deaths, their passing.
This Mazda silver bullet could detonate
A supernova inferno of vehicles.
A collision of worlds.
Hello and goodbye, *ex nihilo.*

Shall I lay my dirt upon your grave?
No. If and when I implode,
This stitcher of contemplations
Will take a lot of people with him,
On the wrong side of right.
But … I will save lives … tonight …

I Don't Talk to Machines

Worship technology? Not me, emoji.
Before bits and bytes, the Luddites had it right.
Now nothing is sacred, Benedictine or green.
You know what I mean? I don't talk to machines.

Find your device where the gadget graveyards lie.
Debris buried in the earth, debris buried in the sky.
Stuck on delete, it all becomes obsolete.
You know what I mean? I don't talk to machines.

Household gods sold to clear: iPod, iVideo, iPhone,
Hosanna on Wi-Fi! With an earbud, I'll never walk alone.
For a troll-free prayer line, call the number on your screen.
You know what I mean? I don't talk to machines.

Forget your password, Skip Ad, Twitter litter. LOL.
It all spells No iDeals. Say nothing faster, $30 an hour.
I don't need voice command, artificial demand.
You know what I mean? I don't talk to machines.

Spyware, malware, watch your underwear.
Speed date for a mate. Toneless aloneness.
Fake art, no heart, add to cart. Upgrade and demean.
You know what I mean? I don't talk to machines.

I'm not a technophobe. My frontal lobe
Just wasn't designed for junk in my earlobe.
Hooked on hazardous taste, you become the waste.
You know what I mean? I don't talk to machines.

Can't talk to people either, texting next to each other.
Dumb thumbs. Can't name the constellations,
But U want 2 B a ★ inside a zoo with 12 million views.
You know what I mean? A cyber latrine, forever 18.

The Golden Mean has always been where it's @,
Not the Consumer Holocaust, or a phishing RAT.
Birds, singing at dawn, automatically turn me on.
The same old scheme. I don't talk to machines.

Say Something to the Camera

Cheesey!

Hi, one eye.
Get my good side.
Don't lie.

Hocus pocus,
Please God,
Come into focus.
No image found.

Too bad the paparazzi
Had not appeared yet on the scene
For a candid zoom-in of a virgin birth in a manger,
Or a mug shot of a messiah crucified between two thieves.
Around 33 AD, or BC?
(Before Cameras).

One click,
And photoshopped, botoxed, face-lifted, nose-jobbed,
Lipsticked, blushed, bleached, airbrushed, perfume-wigged,
Eyebrow-penciled, false-eyelashed, acrylic-nailed, mask-ara'd,
Silicone-implanted, platform pumped, transgendered, wind-machined,
Supermodels come alive.

Don't lose your aura in the agora,
Faceless without a franchise.
We're being watched …
So what is our rating?

Optics in the toilet?
Smile.

Look at me, selfie! Look at me! I love myself so much!
Here in the shallows of Varadero beside pink flamingos!

An instagram, a webcam, a dashcam, a bodycam, a kisscam,
Testify to what I am.

Just for the record,
Cover the lens.
Shutter speed can't catch me.

Sahar From Afar

I can see through
Your discarded veil,
Two distant eyes,
Open to question.
Please excuse my hands,
And their second nature
To console and to adjust.
Each strand of your hair
Exposes so lustrously
The darkest nights in Libya,
Under cover of Allah.

You offer me a date:
A half-bitten Maktoom,
And I share some ice wine,
As we discuss gradualism …
Oblivious to the lunar crescent
Moving toward a closer full moon.

Hoejabi

She danced for Saddam Hussein
As a whirling schoolgirl,
When his books had stood
At attention beside the Qur'an.
The dictator and dropout
Had presented himself,
Unannounced,
To inspect the floor,
And his future.

Today,
In our Music and Literature class,
Wearing a hijab and her Sunni smile,
She knows what Saddam would have done
Concerning her uprisings:
Tapping one running shoe,
At will,
To western swing.

The Confirmed Living

At the campus arena, eleven of us drop our hockey sticks upon centre ice. We need a break from giving 110%. Wherever the sticks slide, we take that side. No referees, no penalties, no goalies, no final scores to tabulate, register, or review; a bunch of slapstick academics continue to instruct in grandiloquent fashion. "Go! Go! Skate! Skate! Shoot! Shoot! Back! Back! Awww, shit!" The puck ducks into the net, and guffaws explode from all over the rink to loosen the rafters.

It's a victory for everyone here to be doing what we love to do, lacing up while on the job. Bodychecking is not permitted. But bobblehead geezers are allowed to check for a pulse after one hour of unstiffening. Performance-enhancing drugs such as Robaxacet and Advil don't provide any superluminal advantage for our shinny fantasies. The faces of aces, we team up with colleagues who have beaten cancer, heart disease, poverty, unemployment, the death of children, the temporary insanity of a marital split, those bouts with Johnny Walker on ice, the free-for-all of strikes, the head shots of grievances, the backstabbing and in-fighting. And! The occasional bad bounce. One 70-year-old, an emeritus winger, surges through another test of stamina with a helmetful of hooray memories. Our blades clomp and stomp back into the dressing room, a fellowship of fit spirits; perspiring, laughing, exuberant!

Come home to a massacre of maples, oaks, pines, poplars, elm and ash, paved over for "a new frontier in better living." As adventurous as a *coureur de bois*, I had bumbled through thick woods, searching for an orange property stake, branches slapping my face. Six months later, dead dreams, *à vendre* signs, now stab neglected lawns and frozen fill, owned by Chinese, Greek, and Nigerian neighbours. Unreal estate. So this is my civilized niche? No vandalism, just a screw-you development built by gougers and saw-toothed boars in a hurry over the winter. Days numbered and amortized, morbid maples languish inside tree wells, dug out to save choked roots. Dying branches hug me with their shade. Foxes, coons, and skunks can feast on crumbled fortune cookies in the trash can. No sign of birds yet this spring, just decayed leaves and dirty snow. Will the moon at least come back? In the driveway, blood stains from our cat, accidentally run-over, were cleaned up too hastily. (Beware of children and cats). She had sauntered out to bask in the March sunlight, the days growing longer and warmer. As the car backed up, her yelp for help came with the crushing of bones. Her golden eyes oozed out, two stringy egg yolks. Poor Whizzy, she had been a lost kitten found frolicking in the street, dodging a diesel by a whisker. Cuddleship for over fifteen years, a full life with lots of gravy on top, as a momma cat and mouser, gone in a death spasm of ten seconds; a black beauty that deserved mummification. To propitiate the high-tailed hierophants of Catastrophe, my wife and I thanked her for the daily rewards she had brought us, lightening our burdens with her acrobatic stunts, acupuncture kneading claws, and blinking bedroom eyes. Such a fussy sleeper. We covered her mangled fur with a cloth, neatly placed inside a cardboard box, giving that refined feline a last trip through her favourite rendezvous; stalling traffic to a crawl, a regal sendoff in keeping with her style. To where? To a dignified cremation. To a tale. To lie down beside the wolf and the lamb.

And how is my mother doing? My likeness. I couldn't look at her bloodied face from a two-storey fall. An oxygen mask smothered her screams, rushed *out* of the emergency ward, three days in there, tied down and raving; discharged when she could limp around the bed in her slippers. For now, she rests as dormant as a volcano, her bosom not heaving, napping undisturbed; refusing to enter the death row of nursing homes that await her spite, her anxiety attacks, her "Parkinsonisms," her paranoia, her going deaf, blinded by cataracts, angina strangling her heart. Is this my *mamyte*? An anemic pincushion punctured by life-support invasions. The woman who told me to never throw away anything. On her 80th birthday, her wish was to die.

Go down to the family room. Turn on the TV. Nothing on: nudity, commercials, more gore. Buffy the Vampire courts the walking dead. Something to be: a zombie. Juvenile necrophilia. Snooze to bad news: another suicide bomber on CNN Live. Confirmed dead: 9. Injured: 55. Honestly shocked and appalled: 0. Megadeath, jihad, or mundane world wars: the cadavers, the wounded, the missing, the POW's, all perish into columns of yawning zeros— "close to 300," or "more than 118,000," or "over 60,000,000." Does God count all the deicides for today? Or is God dead too? Every night, on every network it seems, cute pixel people shoot each other for celebrity bucks. Their bang bangs even point at the viewer. Don't dive under the sofa. Watching millennials holding lighted cellphones up high, marching in the streets against mass shootings, can still tug at the guts with hope for unborn generations to press the right power buttons, and to rebel against a global community degenerating into free-fire zones. Otherwise, should the last desensitized *homo sapiens* pay some mind to the post-human pre-mortem? Free the Daedalus in billionaires who dread lying dead and undigitized. Let them purchase wings of nitrogen to malinger frozen in cryonic immortality, quality time, for a Labyrinthine end of life. Or decode death? A resurrection without insurance, as an alter server, a substrate-independent AI emulation of the brain, and its auto parts, self-replicates: non physicality in non locality. Be sure to save those LED soles. Sex, *la petite mort*, can be conquered in bed. But! Death-certificate dead

_____? Why dwell there today? Every time I pass a cemetery, I look the other way.

Lazy as Lazarus, after another late night, I arose this morning out of the sleep-wake cycle, still a dreamer; a heart still working toward peace, public and private, systole and diastole. And this evening, merry moments sparkle inside the house as erratically as the white calcite bricks outside. Dusk, don't go away, while I savour the sizzle of sockeye sautéed in its own juice, spiced with delicious family chitchat, and a libation with wine from productive 100-year-old vines, Châteauneuf-du-Pape and jazz for incorrigible *bon vivants*. "To a loooooong life!"

An "I love you" from my wife at the end of another day, plus a glass of red wine: both are good for the heart. Inhale, exhale, and hail each millisecond as certification.

We, the confirmed living.

Pocketful of Picks

Guitar Introduction

Listen,
I am more than breathing wood,
More than maple with character,
Flaming as I age.
In ancient Egypt,
I descended
From the rays of *Ra*
Into the hands of poets.
In Africa, I was a gourd shimmering with strings;
In China, a *p'i-p'a* plucked along the Silk Road.
In the deep south of France,
Troubadours found the secret
Voice of seduction in my palette of frets.
In Andalucia, I became a *guitarra* for the commoners,
Next in line for the nobles of Arunjuez.
Bookmatched,
Let me speak
What words cannot say
In spruce and rosewood tones.
Hold me always to your heart,
As I carry history and silence,
And the song of the moment.

This Guitar Doesn't Scream

Django Reinhardt (Light Unbowed)

Born to awaken! He touched off the *Manouche* fire.
Two fingers that belonged to forked lightning,
Two feet that took root anywhere like wild violets,
The wind was his map. The only Gypsy with a future.
Selmer, Wormwood, Les Saintes-Maries-de-la-Mer:
Every spirit gathered to play in his smokey key. Freely.

Joachim Rodrigo (Spain Inside a Guitar)

The braille of a blind pianist composed masterpieces for the guitar—
To be played with the eyes open or closed, seeing with two ears.
Hear a miscarried child in muted strings, in doves evanescing above domes,
Reflected in pools and singing fountains. Was it neuroplasticity?
The motifs discerned in restored palaces. Clouds over Madrid re-imagined.
The music came from where? *Corazon.* The beating heart of time.

Antonio Carlos Jobim (If Brazilian Birds Could Sue)

A Blue Macaw, reduced from Rio to a favela, no longer refrains:
La! La! La! La! La! La! La! La! Boy from Ipanema! I want 10%!
A Scarlet Parrot at the beach flirts with the girls. *Wheeet! Weeeeee!*
No bikini! No bikini! Ttttt. Boobies on top of buses. Go on! Samba plucker,
Steal some melodies from a forest sinfonia of piping Guans and Chachalacas.
A Parakeet tunes up giddily: *A, yo. E, yum. G, it's rum. Sailor, gimme some!*

Wes Montgomery (Higher-Evolved Thumb)

It came natural, that octave thing. Nobody told me it was impossible.
So I did it. I just copied that cat Charlie Christian. Then more cats copied me.
It's a natural thing. I had seven children to support. Boy, that food chain
Kept me dead awake, unloading boxcars, lugging ice, stuck to a welding job,
Then playing gigs all night. But the people really dug my tone. Sure.
These hands can thumb tunes for a living any time. It's a natural thing.

Chet Atkins (High Country)

Ten fingers from Tennessee that sound like twenty, y'all!
This here gentleman with his yakety axe, jazzin' up the agriculture,
Spiffin' up the classical crocks, notes as clean as a mountain stream,
Fresh 'n' *ffft* fast! And jeez, he could even make ya hear colours!
Yup. That Nashville thumbity-thump was really somethin' else.
Too city for the country, too country for the city. Pick yer own.

George Harrison (Hari's Son)

He knew more deities, gave away more money, and dressed better
Than the other millionaire rockers. Beatlemania: have Mersey!
Liverpool lad, son of a bus driver, ahead of his time,
The karma route welcomes a sunburst soundboard of the Lord.
Through a guitar, a sitar, a ukulele, he diminished the darkness
Within the weeping oneness of the world. The Way. Love one another.

Pedal Steel Soliloquy

For Al Brisco

I avoid practicing this outsider among guitars —
This four-legged critter tied to cowboys:
Those beefy fingers pickin' and a-grinnin'
On an Emmons in some honky-tonk oink oink.
Why can't suburban vegans do that?

Recorded evidence proves
That this beast can be played.
Begin with one broken heart,
The most important moving part.
Two hands, preferably accustomed to hard work—
Pickaxe, claw hammer, grappling hooks,
And the grind of the long haul—
Do most of the job unloading glissandi of songs
Across twenty-five frets and ten strings,
Blocked by the palm so a tone bar
Can slant and slur and shimmer tons of vibrato.
Two knees must also cooperate, tightsy-antsy-pantsy,
To pull pitch, harnessed by four
Giddyup-and-go-out-of-tune levers.
Plus the heel and toe must promenade,
One step, two steps, or hover with no steps,
Not getting lost across three pedals to the floor.
(No brakes. Careful. Don't play too fast!)
While the right foot, the feeler,
Delicately drives a volume pedal for that crying sound,
So fluid and gorgeous, if tears had tones.
Thanks, all you Hanks and Buds and Buddys.

I'll lay my hands on this silent steel,
This Birdseye Maple covered with dust,
Giving me dirty looks.
When all seems gloomy
Outside this room,
I sit down and slide on a blue sky.
Alone and high.

Phantom Ohm

My subliminal channel selects Bach's *Prelude in C*,
As I drive through profanity in the city. The radio off.
A phantom ohm.
What comes after deep, deeper, deepest?
The pain of hearing my mother on her deathbed:
The horrible gurgle of aspiration pneumonia,
As water saturated the airways in her lungs;
The noise of the nebulizer with its almost inaudible persistent hum;
The morphine protocol easing the ebbing of her voice into silence;
The tacitness of her last breath, peaceful.
Those sounds interrupt my day too,
While life interferes with grieving,
And the hymn I now sing at her grave
In harmony with those phantom ohms.

Hearing Voices

"Son, it looks like you got the blues real bad."
—Charlie Biddle

I hear voices across
The Delta to Niagara
The maple that whispers to the magnolia
The dust that accents the air

I hear voices from
Beale St. to Peel St.
As deep as indigo that dances
On snow or inside a flame

I hear voices from the heart
Hard lives hard loves
Touch gloves

I hear voices in the talking drum
Of dreams to come
Graves speaking on

Wherever my tongue slides
Inside your ear or mouth
You will hear my voice
The Blues

I promise you a ride

The Oscar Peterson Line

Tout l'monde ascende!
Let's go retro through the metro.
Just sing a song
And get on for free,
Sittin' and-a-rockin'
Or standin' and-a-swingin,'
A happy feeling,
Floor to ceiling.
Take your ticket
Through the wicket
For a magic time.
Hop on to the Oscar Peterson line.

Well, there's ol' Rufus handin' out his roses.
In his Paradise, the door never closes.
And save a seat for those two ma'ams:
Rosa Parks and Harriet Tubman—
Man, she's just bubblin' at home on the run,
Railroadin' under the ground again;
As Ms. Angélique
Speaks through a fire,
Burnin' in the spire;
And a baritone sax says
Swing with the Royals.
Steal home base,
Mr. Jackie Robinson,
MVP in '49.
Hop on to the Oscar Peterson line.

Shibui, Louie! Now foreign is in.
We got a dash of *duende* on a sunny day.
Salaam and *shantih*. What d'ya say?
We got music on tracks
That don't talk back.
The pull of gospel
To stay connected.
Mississippi, Mississauga,
And I miss you Montréal!
Little Burgundy pedigree.
Memories never stop.
Je vous aime. You are mine.
Hop on to the Oscar Peterson line.

Dead But Still Ahead

Miles Davis.
When I first heard *Kind of Blue*,
I became kind of less green.
My underaged fingers stretched out as far as 52nd Street
To untangle those colossal bitonal jazz chords—
Just as Miles was embalming jazz
As "museum music."

Then I saw him live at the Montréal festival:
A pulsar pushing the range of his red horn,
In a spacey cantos of electron syncopation,
Higher than the fireworks.

And keeping me up tonight, here he is again,
Like his paintings of dancing wraiths,
A treble clef wearing shades.
Not enough hours to catch up with
The embouchure kiss of his ballads;
The "So What," and the Gigawatt,
From so many Miles and Miles ago …

Distingué Traces

I wish I could have reserved one inch
On the piano chair of Duke Ellington,
As he composed *In My Solitude*;
Or to have sat in while *Satin Doll*
Rolled off the fingers of Billy Strayhorn.
The Duke and Swee' Pea: a match parfait.
Who wrote what note to subtract, or ad lib,
In your own distinct way?

Thelonious on the House

Flatten Manhattan
Into fifths
Capture
Midnight
Widen space
Extemporize
Sliding foot
Striding hand
Signature ring
Bejazzled eyes

Shake Rag

Who was Elvis impersonating?
The negroes of Tupelo.
In the shack town of Shake Rag,
Tee Toc unlocked the blues for the boy with sideburns,
Turning Elvis loose, a weathercock before a storm;
The choirs of maids, cooks, merchants, seamstresses, sharecroppers,
And gandy dancers who sang at the Rising Star Baptist churches,
Where Elvis would eavesdrop near a window in his Jericho,
Before the walls and Colored Only signs came tumbling down;
The crotches and yass-yasses who wiggled their bait in juke joints;
The black and white hands who stole from the same bosses;
The same dark stomachs starving for the same taste
Of chitlins and fried squirrels.

Elvis Aaron Presley,
Truck driver and baritone bridge,
Picked up the South and delivered it to the world:
The lows of lonely streets,
To peace in the valley,
To the blueness of blue Hawai'i.

The Blues Queue

For the left-overs:
The white trash,
Safe in their skin,
Five tattoos,
Four pigments,
No class.

Try on dignity,
Fought and paid for,
As neat as the bow tie of Satchmo,
Or the silk suits of B.B.
See the blues in shined shoes.

Blind Boy Beginner,
Learn how to play
Them easy licks
In less than a week
(With a free CD),
Faster than a mechanical
Cotton picker.

Don't cuss
In the back of an airbus.
Go to hell with your death-metal derivatives.
Guttural goons assault, bash, bite, bend, thrash and strangle strings.
Guitars hang in shops
Like lynched bodies.

America woke up this morning.
Yonder in Washington,
Get your Blue Room right,
The one that takes you higher,
A hoot above the South Lawn.

Step right up.
Snap fingers.
Fix debts,
Not snacks.
The White House is now rockin' 'n' ruling
With smiling blacks.

A Mighty Fortress Is Our Bach

A polyphony of too many notes,
Too many children,
Too many heavens.
Are we there yet?

Abstain from holy hypocrisy,
The unending ritual of religious wars: abort them.

Abstain from patriarchal pillars that keep out women —
Even nuns in ecstasy.

Abstain from sermons that denounce materialism
Under gilt vaults.

Abstain from exegetical fallacies,
And the call of delusion.

Abstain from pedophile undertones,
And be gay.

But never ever abstain from Johanne Sebastian Bach,
The sound of light,
The well-tempered cantor.
Each sharp, each flat, each interval, declaims:
Music is me.
Do-Re-ME!

Bees and Halos

A circling bee,
A sweet thought.
Is that a hive?
Or a holy city?
Swarms turn hexagons
Into honeycombs so infallibly.

Music for open ears:
The pop and fizz of ginger ale—
Accompanied by the zest of a zinging bee.
Allegro go go go!
Change buckwheat into honey for the hottest healingest tea.
Our keepers.

We and the bee
Are light,
Slowed down.
Longitude,
Latitude,
Bee attitude.

Melody and Lunacy

Pierrot Lunaire saved music
From "the death of tonality."

Then along came the flow of *Moon River*,
Conducted by Henri Mancini.

Pure and Applied

H_2O will always be water
To bring out the flavours
In the controlled burn
Of single-malt VR 1 heat receptors,
From throat to chest to liver transplant,
For devotees of good Scotch and bad breath,
Aging while trying to pronounce
Glentauchers, Laphroaig, Uigeadail.
Gang the gither acetaldehyde and bog swallowers all!

100 mgs of thujone
Will always be too stoned
For any *foufou*
To fly out of body
Via the Green Fairy.

And 1.75 litres of Jägermeister,
Tamed by 473 mls (medicinal leaps) of Red Bull,
Yes sir eee'd by froth that sings effervescently,
Served in a yard glass,
Chilled colder than the tears of a communist,
Will always be zero gravity,
Under the periodic table,
And over a cliff.
Bottom's up!

Dragon Fruit

Antioxidant emperor of the fruit bowl
Spiky leaf punker pear
Scent of radish in rouged skin
Lycopene fire
Slice and hold a galaxy as a prize
Cactus seed dark stars
Dispersed to spoon out
Across the pitahaya nebula
Sing with a mouthful
Melonicious mysterious
A royal treat
A crime to eat

This Putt Reads Poetry

This putt couldn't make it through *Leaves of Grass*.
This putt breaks trochaic
                      then skips off line by five iambic feet.
This putt practices a pendulum swing, a repeated pleasure, all iteration.
This putt loves the ping of onomatopoeia, the rattle in a cup. (Quiet please.)
This putt is worth one million dollars. *OHHHHHHHHHHHHHHHHHHH!!!*
This putt … yips … and … hangs … on … to … the … lip …
This putt is as simple as a simile like the pressure that sends a man to his knees.
This putt stresses hyperbole and swears that the hole moved.
This putt uses Planck's Constant for ball oscillations, downhill, allegorical pull.
This putt was sunk by a chimpanzee.
This putt can't stand rhymes by amateurs: "Drive for show, and putt for dough."
This putt, ironically, rolled further than the foozled drive.
This putt opines that Visiball glasses, and finding assonance are both asinine.
This put can't picture a hole as a bucket, and hulas out, dropping metaphors.
This putt robs—dashes—diphthongs on aerated; European; Zoysia.
This putt has a mind of its own and should be shot for personification.
This putt wonders why the anonymous ever hit rocks into rabbit holes?
This putt was flung into a lake with angry joy. What an oxymoron!

Resistance Training

Do sit-ups, push-ups, curl-ups, deadlifts.
Balance the body, the mind, and the bank account.
Squat, centred, swinging you-bet-I-sweat kettlebells.
Burn at the core, the weight of the world reduced on a stability ball.
Walk much taller, endorphins dancing, fully alive on any scale.
Gene expression Herculean. A sexy sexagenarian.

Don't hang the head in a gallow's position for hours;
Dishevelled, sedentary, stiff as the spine of a hardcover book.
Counter the urge to bemoan the human condition,
A glum cerebrum held up by one finger, cigarette smoke, pills, alcohol.
Resist writers reading to other writers,
Tombstones staring at other tombstones.

First Licence

"There's the ash tree.
There's the elm tree.
There's the maple tree—
And there's the poetree!"

"Everywhere!"
My eight-year-old rookie
Spins and cartwheels,
As we pitch and catch
A baseball and swap repartee.

This happiness
For postmodern novices:
A baton I never want to let go
In the relay race against time.

Stray Birds for Unwanted Children in a Lost World

"Birds are probably the greatest musicians to inhabit our planet."
—Olivier Messiaen

Hermit Thrush, Hear This

Conshushness
Our Common Loner
Takes a vowel of silence
Two tears old
Scripples on a window
Mama's nail polish a pen
A scribe straight out of the crib
Jots on a sunrise
To innerstand the outside
That same child locked inside
A greying body
Looks for the ineffable
The whatchamacallit
The bird of absurdity
Voiceless *pssst*
Strokes pundamentals
Pidgins
To sing with the uncaught swans
Of Weltanschauung
Where angels wash
His birthmurk
A red scare
It won't go away
Not a stork bite
Let's distinguish it
Doctor X says
With hex rays
A handy capper machine
Butchers the carpus meat
A clipped wing on a fledgling

A misfit in any armour
If the Luftwafflers
Had won the war
Dropping swastikaka
Everywhere
Just following disorders
Like that Fokker Göring
Our Common Loner
Would be asleep
In youthanasia
Lullaby booties
Sent to limbo
Bunglekind for Himmler
And his SS white coats
Injectors of phenol
Into suspected invalids
Who belong in lumpen gas chambers
EichmannMengeleBormanBarbieStreicher
FrickFrankKeitelSpeerRibbentropKaltenbrunner
The arschgeburts
The cooked goose steppers
Blitzed medals of denial
Goebbel gobbles
Guilty of rhymes against humanity
Adwarf Hitler
That little bustard
Mein Koomph'd himself
A tremoring Deutsch Hand Über Alles
Kernel von Stuffinburger
Heil'd as a no arm
One-eyed
Two-hearted
Three-fingered nice assassin

Dressed himself with his teeth
Plucky valkyrie
Carry on
Nothing to hold onto
Lili Marlene in the rain
No light from Buchenwald
Puke on wall
Lampshades
Made of bluh
Camphide
No superior solution
From über boobers
To remove
One strawberry hemangioma
O mama
It could have just faded away
With the stench of war
·And the crash
Into the blazoned pyre
Of a barbecued Reichsadler
Feh
Time
Where does it fly
Ask the keepers
The swifts
And the *Zeitgeists*
Fasten your chuckles
This is going to be
A long trope
A roamin' alphabet
Used abused reclused
News'd sports'd weather'd
A shell opens up

A cherubim's wings
Our Common Loner
Churns up a budgie breakfast
Of seeds berries veggies
The almighty smoothie
A Cardinal whistles epistles
Birdiebirdiebirdie
Whatdyaeatwhatdyaeatwhatdyaeat
Pewpewpewpewpew
Good morning measuring cup
What's left unfulfilled
Circa this scoop
Of a second
Be the best father figure
On two legs
Find peace in a niece
Her buy a logical dad
Ran away after her birth
Now her open arms seek
A huggy wuggy
A lift ooopalai
A taxi ride on Uncle Dad's back
They sing on a swing together
Or chortle with cross-eyed
Spoon-on-nose silliness
I'm a Hornbill
I'm a Hornbill
Gonna eat you up
Omnomnomnomnomn
Who can touch the ceiling
The Higgs boson
Makes it big today too
Adorable particle

Charging with zero spin
Smashing Spinoza and Vatican II
And the shy first mover
The *Lux Æterna* before all suns
And photons and protons
And plasma stringing
Leaping leptons and years
On and on and on
To the Tao of now and then
Precambrian micro orgasms
Suppernatural selection
A jaw a claw a papilla
Were is will be in no time
Platonic and tectonic
Feathers in the ether
Norns and Avatars
Vultures and undertakers
Paratroop the colours
Of comeuppance
A royal Turkey
Sits on an Ottoman
Birds and bats
Pose for da Vinci's studies
Flighty graphomaniacs
Think ink and quills
Syllables congregate
Flocksinanitchynihilipileofdefecation
Darwin wins
Ape shape skull
Our pal in genesis
Wingy forelimbs
And fishy philtrum
Smilin' 'n' a-morphin'

The inhuman race
Related to cutthroat Archaeopteryx
Or the egg-stealing
Raven that roosts
Atop a totem pole
Meegwetch
Pro creators
Split or bind
Then die
Arctic Tern
Master of migration
Overturn the urn
Life into afterlife
Can't imagine
Being breathless
Without a flight
We're back
We're back
Those honkers
Canada Geese
Wave hello
Harbingers of winter
Transporters of spring
Ushering in maple seed whirlybirds
Our Common Loner wheels with them
Through an early bloomer morning
Dead cells cleansed
Exfoliated revitalized
Driving a sedan
Washed spic and span
Attuned to byways
Potholes pylons koans
Beding bedang bedung

The whoosh of the wind
Widens wintered fingers
Arm wrestling
Out the window
Lift and drag
The sun a blazing bellybutton
Puts on a hydrogen
And helium light show
Out of the lilacs
Of Coteau-du-Lac
A Barn Swallow
Scrapes by the windshield
As if on fire
Whew
You're not a phoenix petite friend
News crumbs on the air waves
Ration all eyes in the evening
How a plane had enginegested
A family of geese
What panache
Bird strikes
Hurt everyone
Building dings
Or airport bloodbathos
No Accipiter Radar
Cheap cheap
Diners in recliners
Overcrowded conzoomers
Munch on defrosted
Overcrowded chickens
Homo Jetseticus
Their expiry date
When will it arrive

Frequent flyers
Shoo
Smokers
Shoo
Disease carriers
Shoo
Security checks
Shoo
Can't recognize a cuckoo
Shoo
Can't mate for life
Shoo
Who is the birdbrain
It's not over
Plover
The mind
Has a way out and in
Transcendence so scant
Dormant
Head
Under
Wings
A nod
To the numinous
The cry
Of one Loon
Diving
Into its own
Reflection
As calm as a psalm
The lament of the Hermit Thrush
Delivers the Gabriel message
For today and tomorrow

Put that on our calendar
Upwardly mobile
Mountain retreaters
The Chough
Knows when
To say enough
Look no further for
Firdaws Bhuva Loka Kumwamba Tian Shamayim
Not birds but the taxonomy of heaven
That six inches
Between our ears
Our will
And the Whip-poor-will's
No more vertical dives
Due to devilish oilygarchs
Birds sing in the air
Whales sing in the water
But folks
No longer sing anywhere
Not even on the back porch
The rant of a raptor
Goes unheard
Forty stories
Above a crane operator
In a secular and sanctimonious
Bleepin' 'n' beepin' metropolis
Where a nest
Upon an office tower
Hallows such tiny rapture
Cerulean Warbler
Stimulate the encomium
Owl and Shearwater
Acolytes of starlight

Enspirit our hunt for
THE GRAND UNIFIED TRUTH OF EVERYTHING
LARGER THAN GOVERNMENT FUNDING
1, 2, 3, 4, 5, 6 senses not enough
But let's hear it for the terra-ra-ra
Of radio telescopes most high
The oldies on cosmic microwave background radiation stations
Audioooooooooooooooooo too hollow to lure the lyre of Apollo
Or the Wholly One Orchestration
A Big Bang
Ain't so hot
The song of singularity
Intuit it
The *troolooloolooloo*
Of a black hole
Transmutes into the *tweet tweet*
Of a Goldfinch as a paraclete of paradox
The contrary motion of a Hummingbird
Flying backwards
53 wingbeats per second
Whirs up a stellular calliope
Tik tik tik tik tik
Immaculate
Peewit
NASA can't spy
The why in the sky
The neura loorah loorah of love
Namaste have a nice day
We are ecumenical nuclei
Mass light energy
Prana ki chi
Third Eye or Trinity
Apes to apse

Both faith and reason
Are two feats to stand on
Be true to altruism in you
In dolphins in leopards in birds
What came first
The aureole or the oriole
How do curlews do it
Traversing arctic nights
No stopovers no autopilot
Beating the darkness
The wingspan of one thank you
Can travel a long way too
At Point Pelee in knee-high snow
Our Common Loner sings to the songbirds
That didn't fly south before Decembrrrrrr
I am a flame poof
He fans out shivering arms
And displays his colours
Silver hair not worth a dime
Blue eyes twinkling with a boyish shine
Pink complexion white as an albino crow
Red nose rosey from rosacea
A sacred clown
He stumbles through a flightless *jeté*
For the attention of one Grey Jay
Bardwatching
His Passerine airs
The stillness bids him
To relinquish the binoculars
And to envision
The untold
A peregrination of grinning atoms
Following extinction

A shot at apocatastasis
Through a wormhole
The Dodo returns
To perch beside a black butterfly
The Réunion Solitaire comes back
To sunbathe with seagulls
On a soccer field
End to end
The Imperial Woodpecker
In all its impeccability
Drills on deadwood
Unmuffling conundrums
Dusky Seaside Sparrows arise
Into unfamiliar morning light
While Laughing Owls laugh again
The warblers the chatterers the babblers
That disappeared with the timbres
And the winds of the wetlands
Materialize out of a morass
Of forget-me-nots
Shedding their deaths
As naturally as moulting
Passenger Pigeons
Settle upon the shoulders
Of commuters at a bus terminal
Sky trains and self-driving cars ahead
Carriages buggies and drays behind
A where are we moment
Dovetails
Borne again
Upon the lifelines
Of unwanted children
The phlox in commotion

No species more special
Than any other
Kingfisher or fakir
Great Auk
Or incorruptible saint
No age in time more golden
Than daybreak
Peace
An olive tree
Grows inward
And outward
To touch all horizons
Observant chirp goer
Our Common Loner
Whittles his strophes
A whispering craft
Hushing the ash trees
While rows of cedars
Slow down the summer hours
The pleasures of stillness
The poplars not trembling
The cumulus not moving
The lacecaps lulling a dragonfly
On the hydrangeas of home
When suddenly wow wow wow wow wow
A bird wave darkens the lawn
Sends the cat hiding under the hostas
A chittering frenzy
Hundreds thousands
Beaucoup de birdeees
Forage off sodding
Carpets of greenery
Unrolled just for them

More creatures of the air
Than seeds in the feeder
They curtsy and gorge
On corn millet wheat and milo
A coalition of crows blackbirds
Blue jays cardinals juncos grackles
Finches sparrows robins chickadees
Swooping from a cloud formation
The beard of Zeus
Splitting S
Speaking *eeeek*
Awk words
Conference calls
Of squeaky flybys
Québecois tui tui tui
No left wing
Right wing
Partisan divides
Unanimous
Diplumacy
Male blackbirds
Manly hippity hopkins
Cover their red badges
Beaks upraised triumphant
Voracious insectivorous
The grub inspectors have arrived
The chubby checkers
The famished eyes
The fleet feet
The 1-metre sprinters
Scurry ravenous
Through Kentucky Bluegrass
To gab gob colonies

Of dainty ants
Uncovering beetle
Mosquito larvae
Marxist millipede
Hideouts
One nuthatch
Pickpeckpocks
A maple trunk
Upside down
A circle dance with itself
Darting away *we we we we we*
Skylarks never seen before
Gossip on the patio
Ipipipip pep talks
Tails twitch in semiquavers
Ambassadors at the door
While home wreckers
Those Jumbo Crows
Heavy as crowbars
Weigh themselves
On an eavestrough
Idlers
Whap wings
Along the lattice
Of a wobbly fence
Wo wo legato legs
Yakkers
Ree-bee-ooo recitatives
Lilting the cosmos
Birds birds birds
Beads beads beads
Aves aves aves
Chaplets above

Interspecies exultation
Our jaws agape
A divine comedy
Is happening here
Now in the present indicative
Never to hunger for illusion
To immanentize the eschaton
Trapped by the lid of language
The snare that anthropomorphizes
God
Him
Down
To
Our
Size
The atheism spectrum
No soul (male or female)
Bow to a black hole
A bottomless collection basket
Of lost light
Reductionism
Who yes *who*
Can prey as gracefully
As the owl in the darkest night
The *om mani padme hūm* of emptiness
Where a bodhisattva and an agnostic
Burnish and erase the jewel of being
Within a quantum temple of uncertainty
Counterpoint the observed and the unobservable
As Orion chases the Pleiades across winter skies
While an underground Collidor
Pursues a causeless Creator
A fugal gulf

Each human being possesses
The power to work miracles
When they can transform hate
Into forgiveness
Jubilation
Find the demon
In eudemonics
The indeterminate
Makes us all sound like idiots
The parrot says
To the awesome amazing cool guy
I can talk can you fly
The caw of a crow
A corvid Caruso
Skids down a snow-fluff roof
On a risible rideable tailboggan
Jolly follies
A hatched athlete
Our Common Loner
As a featherweight totflot
Would yell yippee I can fly
Taking off from the garage roof
Arms flapping hurry hurry up
To flop into a snow-in-the-boots bank
Scaring away the sparrows
So air unworthy
Wearing the red white and blue
Of the Frenchmen with Flying Elbows
Winter wasn't winter without winning
Stanley Cup parades grew along with you
A rite as predictable as tulips
Popping up *voila* every spring
The entire providence *flyé*

Skatemark flight patterns
Melted slushily on hoser ice
A backyard paradise
Sports versus everything else
Reveries in centre field curved
Around the seams of a baseball
As summer slid into a sandlot
The thunking thrill
Of a diving catch
A game gone into extra meanings
Congratulatory hand slaps
Knuckle bumps
Even from the ump
Teams named after birds
Blue Jays Cardinals Orioles
Something to do with spirit
Intangibles at play
Being in the zone
The élan of a golf swing
As if gripping a bird in your hands
Then swooshing away
As a Top Flite ball
Soars over water
To alight on an elevated green
Another birdie opportunity
Bird songs
Never go out of style
Palely imitated by
Trills on flutes or strings
Toots and hoots
On piccolo or horn
Tweetquency harmonics
Piddly rimshot paradiddles

Peter out duplicating
Sapsucker staccato
Perkkkkk cussion
The Trumpeter Swan
Doesn't trumpet
Or lip sync
Sure of its organs
It tutors sincere ears
Not artifice or farce
The vox humana
How quacky
The Nightingale
Requires no Auto-Tune
Not transfigured either
By a mystic chord
The concerto for ego
Piano tux and tails
Or a pastorale
Rapt in aerial violins
Above a lea
Range nowhere close
To the mellifluous mile
Of a meadowlark
Awakening the grassland
Or a robin riffin' unruffled
On a power line
Check out the cap and goatee
Of a chickadee
Dee-dee-dee-ing
Along a marquee
If you can't carry a melody
Then you karaoke
Popcorn for the masses

And the mongrel gulls
Press an ear
To a recycling bin
Mashups moshpits
The bad taste of the minute
Fire the Band-in-a-Box
And build a birdhouse
Don't feed the MIDI
The Mockingbird
The Magpie
The Lyrebird
The onomatopolyglots
Enamour the heart of a ladybird
By mimicking a chainsaw a tractor
Or a farmer who speaks Farsi
Beating the B-Box boys
No special FX
No sampling
No Mills Brothers vocalics
Just a syrinx
Inimitable endowment
Sunday every day
Whenever those avian
Joy bringers are around
A chorale as supernal
As any that caught the ear
Of St. Ambrose or Gregory
Ornitheology
In the heart-shaped
Flight path of a Godwit
Every National Park endures
As sacrosanct as Noah's ark
Seek out the peacelords

The luminous treetop singers
The water skimmers and hymners
The Hooded Mergansers
The serendipitous Sandpipers
The right riverend herons
That keep us waiting
Our Common Loner lingers
At Parc des Rapides
Just to hear the *yeahyeahyeah*
Of a Blue-Billed Gadwall
Just to behold
The ruby throated
Green eared
Chestnut crowned
Heralds that sustain our gaze
In this orphan dimension
Beginnings and endings
That remain non-negotiable
The scent of Easter lilies
Revealed the presence
Of his mother's incorporeal self
On the way to her funeral
On a cold March morning
No flowers in the car
All windows closed
Her *dvasia* intervening for five witnesses
To assure that she was in a good place
And to mitigate their fear of death
Ah to glide on the back
Of a Gandaberunda
Deathless
Rearing two heads
Looking both ways at once

Beyond words and numbers
All figured out before crossing
Or to loopy loop with starlings
In their ominous murmuration
A black shroud
Folding and unfolding
Grace out of panic
When the falcon strikes
Go too just as freely
Within the same
Design of finality
The whorling shadow
Fingerprint of I
Disembodied
Through the unerring
Turning of time
This stream for strays
This scrum of selves
This oddest of plaudits
Reach out
For the song of a vagrant bird
Flitting into the unknown
Hermit Thrush
Cantillate assertively
Your antiphon to oblivion
You're me
You're me me me
You're me me me

Acknowledgements

Thanks to the big hearts:

Irena, Raimonda, and Rimantas Bojazinskas: keepers of the family tree.

Antonio D'Alfonso for his encouragement of so many minority voices throughout the decades.

Antanas Sileika for putting up with my spinning bear hugs as his house guest; and for his comradeship in Vilnius, Sodus, Chicago, Montréal and Toronto.

Joe Silverman for his joviality and erudition as a polymath; an astronomer and global traveller who is wearing out every turnstile on this planet.

Fr. Paulius Mališka for his support of this free spirit.

About the Author

Literature

Raymond Filip was born in Lübeck, Germany, 1950. He has written 5 books of poetry, as well as a collection of short stories entitled *After the Fireworks* (Guernica Editions). In 1995 he won the QSPELL/QWF poetry award for his book *Flowers in Magnetic Fields* (Guernica Editions). His poems have appeared in major anthologies such as *The Penguin Treasury of Canadian Popular Songs and Poems* edited by John Robert Colombo (Penguin 2002); *The New Canadian Poets 1970-1985* edited by Dennis Lee (McClelland & Stewart 1985); and *Canadian Poets of the 80s* edited by Ken Norris (House of Anansi 1983). He is also included amongst a choice blend of Montréal authors in the coffee-table book entitled *Closer to Home* (Vehicule Press 2009). A former Québec contributing editor to "Books in Canada," (1981-1987), his articles and reviews have appeared in close to 100 magazines and periodicals. His work has been translated into French, Spanish, Italian, and Lithuanian.

Music

Raymond Filip has performed his "say then play" recitals across Canada, parts of the United States, and in Europe. His early collection of songs, *Playing the Poet*, came out in 1989. He has composed the music for two plays by David Fennario: *Neil Cream* (1991) and *Banana Boots* (1995). His music has been broadcast by the CBC, as well as on Lithuanian radio, and local stations. His song "Angels" was covered by Diane Heatherington; as well as performed by the *La Voix Junior* star Denice Sophia Gurrea accompanied by the *Aušros Vartai* choir.

Organizer

From 1981-1986, he hosted *Pluriel*: the first public bilingual reading series in Montréal, sponsored by the Canada Council. It was Canada's finest hour which featured writers such as Canadian nationalist poet Al Purdy reading together with Québecois separatist poet Gaston Miron. (The French won all the poetry *soirées* and the English won all the referendums!)

Miscellaneous

His work was published clandestinely in Soviet-occupied Lithuania throughout the 1980s within the pages of *Sietynas*. He was invited to perform during the *Poezijos pavasaris* tour of 1993, following independence. In 1989, his poems were dramatized, along with those of other writers such as Nobel laureates Czeslaw Milosz and Joseph Brodsky, in the off-Broadway production in New York entitled *Etched in Amber*. In 2018, the translated version of *Etched in Amber/Irėžta gintare* was staged in Kaunas and Vilnius, as part of the centenary celebrations of Lithuanian independence.

Printed in January 2019
by Gauvin Press,
Gatineau, Québec